Rookie
biographies™

Jackie Robinson

By Wil Mara

Consultants
Nanci R. Vargus, Ed.D.
Primary Multiage Teacher
Decatur Township Schools, Indianapolis, Indiana

Katharine A. Kane, Reading Specialist
Former Language Arts Coordinator
San Diego County Office of Education

Children's Press ®
A Division of Scholastic Inc.
New York   Toronto   London   Auckland   Sydney
Mexico City   New Delhi   Hong Kong
Danbury, Connecticut

Designer: Herman Adler Design
Photo Researcher: Caroline Anderson
The photo on the cover shows Jackie Robinson.

Library of Congress Cataloging-in-Publication Data

Mara, Wil.
   Jackie Robinson / by Wil Mara.
      p. cm. — (Rookie biographies)
Includes index.
Summary: Brief text chronicles the life of the Hall of Fame baseball player who,
in 1947, became the first African American to play for a major league team.
   ISBN 0-516-22520-0 (lib. bdg.)   0-516-27336-1 (pbk.)
   1. Robinson, Jackie, 1919-1972—Juvenile literature. 2. Baseball players—United
States—Biography—Juvenile literature. 3. African American baseball players—
Biography—Juvenile literature. [1. Robinson, Jackie, 1919-1972. 2. Baseball
players. 3. African Americans—Biography.] I. Title. II. Series.
   GV865.R6 M37 2002   '
   796.357'092—dc21

                                    2001008319

CHILDREN'S PRESS, AND ROOKIE BIOGRAPHIES™, and associated
logos are trademarks and or registered trademarks of Grolier Publishing
Co., Inc. SCHOLASTIC and associated logos are trademarks and or
registered trademarks of Scholastic Inc.
1 2 3 4 5 6 7 8 9 10 R 11 10 09 08 07 06 05 04 03 02

Do you like to play baseball?

Jack Roosevelt Robinson did.
He was so good that he became
a Hall of Fame baseball player.

He was born in Cairo, Georgia,
on January 31, 1919.

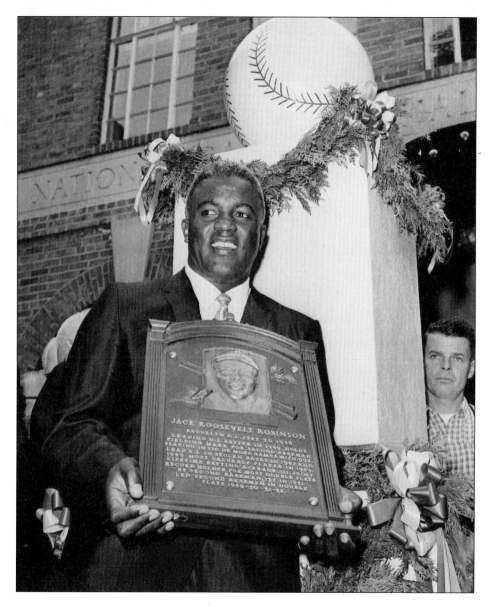

6

Jackie Robinson loved sports. In college, he was on football, basketball, baseball, and track teams.

In 1945, Robinson began playing baseball for a team called the Kansas City Monarchs.

9

The Monarchs were a team
in the Negro League.

There was another baseball league called the Major League. African Americans were not allowed to play in the Major League in those days.

12

In August of 1945, Robinson met a man named Branch Rickey. Rickey ran a team in the Major League. His team was called the Brooklyn Dodgers.

Rickey asked Robinson to be the first African American to play in the Major League. Robinson said yes.

On April 15, 1947, Jackie Robinson ran onto the field to play first base for the Dodgers.

15

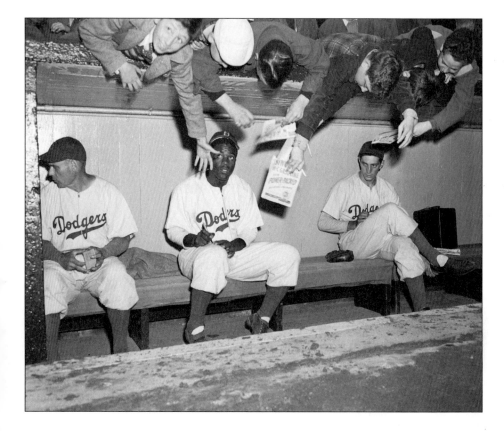

Most baseball fans cheered for Robinson. But some booed. They did not like having an African American play in the Major League.

Robinson kept playing anyway.
He worked hard to be a good
baseball player.

In his first season, he was the Major League's Rookie of the Year. Two seasons later he became the Most Valuable Player.

Still, many people kept doing and saying mean things to Robinson. They would write nasty letters to him and call him names. Some of these people were his own teammates!

22

After awhile, Robinson began to stand up for himself. A lot of people admired him for doing this.

Robinson played his last season in 1956. By then, more African Americans were playing in the Major League.

Robinson died on October 24, 1972. He was 53 years old.

Robinson did a great thing with his life. He made a difference. Thanks to Jackie Robinson, African Americans are able to play baseball in the Major League.

29

Words You Know

baseball

Brooklyn Dodgers

football

Major League

Most Valuable Player

Negro League

Branch Rickey

Jackie Robinson

31

Index

About the Author

Wil Mara has written over fifty books. His works include both fiction and nonfiction for children and adults. He lives with his wife and three daughters in northern New Jersey.

Photo Credits

Photographs © 2002: AP/Wide World Photos: 26 (Doug Kanter), 19, 31 top left (Marty Lederhandler), cover (John J. Lent), 5, 6, 9, 11, 15, 18, 30 bottom left, 30 top right, 30 bottom right, 31 bottom right; Corbis Images/Bettmann: 16, 21, 22, 25; Masterfile: 3, 30 top left (Zoran Milich); National Baseball Hall of Fame Library, Cooperstown, N.Y.: 10, 12, 29, 31 bottom left, 31 top right.